Just Add One: The Shortest Self-Help Book you will Ever Read

By Tyler Taggart

© 2021
FNASM

Edited by Dawn M. Wooten

© Copyright 2021 by Tyler Taggart - All rights reserved.

The following book is designed to help individuals with goal-setting and improving their lives. This book is not meant to replace advice of professionals, such as mentors, counselors, or medical personnel.

The transmission, duplication, or reproduction of any of the following work including specific information will be considered an illegal act regardless of if it is done electronically or in print. This extends to creating a secondary or tertiary copy of the work or a recorded copy and is only allowed with the express written consent from the Publisher. All additional rights reserved.

Additionally, the information in the following pages is intended only for informational purposes and should not be considered a psychological or medically based treatment.

Contents

Preface: The truth about most self-help books 1
Chapter 1: Define Your Goals 4
   The WOOP Method 7
   Lead, Lag, and Score 9
   What Drives Behavior? 13
Chapter 3: How to Design Effective Triggers 20
   Neuroplasticity and the Brain 22
Chapter 4: Just Add One 28
Chapter 5: The Worksheets 32
   Re-Define your Goals 33
   Action Item: Design your Triggers 45
   Action Item: Build Your Scoreboard 46
Resources 50

Preface: The truth about most self-help books

Here is the truth about most self-help books: they are too long and full of fluff. Whether it is because bigger books appear to be more valuable and sell better, or for some other reason, who knows. What we all do know is that they are too long. Additionally, many of them are not immediately actionable. While everyone can get something useful from this book, it will be most enjoyed by people who like to get stuff done. No hours and hours of reading. Get in, get out, get moving.

Just Add One (JAO) is designed to be concise. It will give you specific principles and recommendations on how to take action on each principle. JAO is also intended to be a framework that you can build around your life. It will help you take responsibility for your own results.

This book distills the best of the best from giants such as Tony Robbins and Craig Manning, to lesser-known (but just as important) researchers like Dr. BJ Fogg. There are three things I hope you learn how to do by practicing what is in this book:

1. Set goals in a way that stacks the odds in your favor.
2. Increase your ability to do a task and learn to decrease the required ability for a task by leveraging your most abundant resources.
3. Drive disciplined behavior through designing smart triggers (or prompts).

Set your goals. Design your triggers. Leverage ability. By using this process, you will find that your life gets dramatically better every year. The ultimate purpose of JAO is to help you learn how to set and accomplish goals rapidly and with increasing confidence. As you do so, you will notice a momentum building in your life and you can make progress on goals with excitement.

You will get the most out of this book by doing the following:

1. Read the entire book through one time - beginning to end. Don't take any action on it yet. Get the framework in your mind. Let ideas flow. Now is a good time to take small

notes in the margin, or on your phone or notepad. Keep it flexible though.

2. Restart the worksheet chapter. Start designing the framework in your life. Review the notes you wrote down. Get more concrete about what you want to accomplish. Fill out the worksheets as you go (or find another way to record them on your phone, computer, etc.)

3. Now you are ready to take action. Remember: Just Add One.

Chapter 1: Define Your Goals

"I am so thoroughly convinced that if we don't set goals in our life and learn how to master the techniques of living to reach our goals, we can reach a ripe old age and look back on our life only to see that we reached but a small part of our full potential."
-M Russel Ballard

"When performance is measured, performance improves. When performance is measured and reported, the rate of improvement accelerates." -Thomas S. Monson

There are a thousand pieces of advice about how to set goals, how to not set goals, how to set SMART goals, etc. I'm sure you have heard a lot of it. Before we even get into methods of goal-setting, first we need to discuss the following:

- areas of achievement
- types of goals

Areas of achievement are simple. They are the categories goals fall into. The most common categories are physical, spiritual, mental (education), social, and financial (business). You may find that you have another category you want to place goals in. If so, go for it.

It is best to have one major goal in each category. This will ensure that you keep a balanced approach to life and enjoy living as you work towards your goals. Even though you will have goals in each category, it will be important to focus your attention on only one or two goals for any given three-month period.

Remember, each goal you set will require you to take new actions. Those actions will all require resources from you. Keeping your goals focused on one or two at a time ensures you don't spread any of your resources too thin. Once the actions turn into a habit, the resources required to maintain the habit are greatly reduced, and you can add new goals.

Goals are either task-oriented (good) or ego-oriented (not so good). An ego-oriented goal typically has to do with an achievement:

I want to win a gold medal

This goal is focused entirely on achievement and is ego, or outcome, oriented.

There are two major problems with ego-oriented goals. The first is that in setting this type of goal, you are leaving a lot to chance. You could get sick. Lose a limb. The competition might just be plain better. They could have paid off the refs. Your grandma might have died the day before and you aren't performing well. There are innumerable things that are always out of your control.

In addition to external factors being out of your control, ego-oriented goals are difficult to measure consistently leading up to the goal. They are what is called a lagging indicator. You only know if you have won the gold medal after you have won it. Lastly, ego-oriented goals often leave the goal-setting dissatisfying, and you feel empty soon after achieving the goal.

Now there is a place for these types of goals - they can certainly inspire. However, the better way to set goals is to make them task-oriented. Task-oriented goals look something like this:

I am going to practice ping pong for three hours each day for the next three months

This goal is a *task* that you can perform each day. What's important about it is that it is much more in your control. It only requires discipline and foresight to ensure that this goal is met. At the end of the three months, your skills at ping pong will have improved remarkably - and who knows, you might just win the Olympic ping pong gold medal during the next games.

Don't worry about setting goals just yet - there is a worksheet chapter (Chapter 5) that will help you do that. First, there are three additional goal-setting techniques you need to know: WOOP, lead and lag measures, and building a scoreboard.

The WOOP Method

The WOOP method of goal-setting was developed by Dr. Gabriele Oettingen (2014), a professor of psychology at New York University.

WOOP stands for Wish, Outcome, Obstacle, Plan. The method is simple and powerful.

The "wish" is your goal. What is the meaningful wish, dream, goal, or desire that you have? Next is the outcome. What will be the result or feeling that you have when you achieve the goal (wish)? Third, is Obstacle. What obstacles might you face when attempting to reach your goal? Fourth, is Plan. What plan of action will you take to overcome the previously stated obstacle? Three and four can be repeated as many times as needed.

When using WOOP to inform your goal-setting, it will look something like this:

> *Wish*: I want to cut my body fat by 30 pounds
> *Outcome*: I will feel incredibly healthy, sexy, full of energy, and confident. I will also be significantly healthier and won't need my blood pressure medication any longer, which will save me a lot of money!
> *Obstacle*: When I get stressed at work, I like to snack on potato chips that I have at my desk to relax.

Plan: I will buy a bag of almonds and throw away the potato chips. That way when I want to snack I have a healthy thing to snack on
Obstacle: When I get home from work, I don't have the energy to exercise, so I just end up watching TV until it's late then I go to bed.
Plan: Instead of watching TV until it's late, I will limit my TV watching to 1 hour, then spend the rest of the time getting ready for bed early so I can wake up early and exercise in the morning before work when I have more energy.

Lead, Lag, and Score

This is an incredibly powerful concept to understand and is discussed in depth in *The Four Disciplines of Execution* (Huling et.al., 2012). This is an amazing book that I definitely recommend reading.

Lag measures typically describe results. You know you've reached the goal once you've reached the goal. Lead measures are the activities that predict whether or not you will reach the lag measure. Here is an example:

Lag measure: I want to lose 10 pounds in the next 3 months

Lead measure: I will exercise for 45 minutes every day

Lead measure: I will eat only whole foods for the next 3 months

The two lead measures in this case predict the success of the lag measure. You only know if you have reached the lag goal when you step on the scale at the end of the three months. However, the lead measures are something you can measure and report on daily - which leads us to the importance of keeping a scoreboard.

Scoreboards are an incredible tool to help you see your progress. A good scoreboard will have the following qualities:

- Frequently visible (on your bathroom mirror, fridge, desktop, etc.)
- Easy-to-see progress of lead and lag measures at a glance
- Easy to update
- Shared with an accountability partner

In the worksheets section, you can see some examples. If you would like some further details on scoreboards or lead and lag measures, please read *The Four Disciplines of Execution*.

Chapter 2: The Nature of Doing

"Give me a place to stand, and a lever long enough, and I will move the world" -Archimedes

If you have read any number of self-help books, you may recognize a big push to increase motivation. . "Make a dream board." "Find your 'why'." "Put money on the line." Each of these is an example of how you might increase motivation.

But what if motivation doesn't really work? Motivation is fantastic - when you have it. When you don't, life can feel overwhelming, especially if you don't have the necessary tools in place to go beyond motivation. The truth is, motivation is simply one lever that can help move you to action.

When you focus on motivation, you are putting the cart before the horse. Think about it this way - if you are trying to lose weight, what's more motivating? Looking at pictures of people with tan, ripped, beach bodies? Or stepping on the scale and seeing the number 10 pounds less than it was last month? Or fitting into those pants that were getting too tight? When put this way, it's obvious. RESULTS are significantly more motivating.

If results are the motivator, how do you get motivation before you get results? You don't. Motivation comes and goes. There will be days where your motivation is sky high, and other days where you don't even remember what motivation feels like. That's normal.

Because motivation comes and goes, and is primarily affected by your results, there are two additional levers that you should focus on instead. These levers can be pushed and used even when your motivation is low. The levers are discipline and ability.

What Drives Behavior?

Neurologists, psychologists, life coaches, and parents are constantly asking this question. Is it axon connections in the brain that fire in response to stimuli from the environment? Is it a hidden memory of being abused as a child? Something else entirely?

Professor BJ Fogg from Stanford University

(2020) led some early experiments on the original Facebook app marketplace with this question in mind: What drives behavior? He came up with a brilliant thesis called the Behavior Model that turns behavior into a simple formula:

$$B = MAP$$

Behavior = Motivation x Ability x Prompt

Analyze your own behavioral patterns and you will notice that all three of these pieces must be present for a behavior (or action) to occur. Any time you take an action, there must be motivation, even if it is small. You must have the ability to accomplish the behavior. There must also be something that prompts you to act. If any of these three are missing, behavior (or action) does not occur.

There is another significant relationship within this equation - the relationship between motivation and ability. The correlation is straightforward: the less motivation there is, the more ability is required in

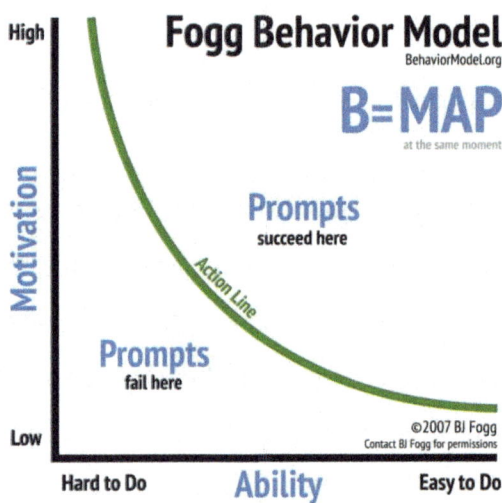

order to reach action. This is shown in Fogg's graph below:

(For more detailed info on BJ Fogg's behavior model, I would recommend checking out his website at www.behaviormodel.org.)

When something prompts you to act, it will only be a successful catalyst for action if the mix of motivation and ability falls above the green "action line." In order to facilitate action, most people focus almost exclusively on the "motivation" lever. Dream boards, personal mantra chants, and listening to music are all examples of how people attempt to increase motivation. However, motivation is not always reliable as a source of "fuel" to get you over the action line and into successful behavioral change. If you truly want to change your behaviors, you need to examine the other lever in this equation: ability.

"That which we persist in doing becomes easier to do, not the nature of the task has changed, but that our power [ability] to do has increased." -Ralph Waldo Emerson

"Do or do not, there is no try." -Yoda

One of the most effective things you can learn to do to reach your goals and improve your life, is to push on the ability lever. To help you understand how to leverage ability, first it is important to understand what I mean by ability. Ability, in this context, is the resources required to accomplish a certain task or goal. Resources usually fall into one of the following categories:

- Physical energy
- Mental energy
- Time
- Money
- Habit (this may seem out of place, but keep reading - it will make sense)

Immediately after you set a goal, identify which resources are going to be required in order to accomplish it. Once you have identified these resources, rank them in order of most abundant to most scarce. Look at the example below:

Goal: Run a marathon
Resources required: physical energy, time, money
Ranked (most abundant first): money, physical energy, time

Depending on your circumstances at the time, the order of most abundant to most scarce will change.

Now it's time to learn about how you can modify the ability required to accomplish a goal. There are two primary ways to modify ability.

First, you can increase your ability by *doing*. The more you do, the more your ability to do increases. The more your ability to do increases, the less motivation is required to perform that same action. This is especially true once the action solidifies as a new habit. By turning a new action into a habit, you dramatically reduce the number of resources required to take that action. Additionally, doing something over and over again creates habit. As habits are created, it reduces the amount of resources required to do the same action in the future.

Modifying ability in this way requires discipline. Discipline to do, over and over again. The more you do, the more your ability will increase and the stronger the habit will become. The discipline to do an action daily is one of the most powerful forces in the world.

The second way to reduce the ability required is to modify the action itself. This is done by breaking the action into small parts in order to decrease the ability required to perform any part of the task.

For example, perhaps you have a goal to learn Mandarin Chinese. The ability, or resources, required to learn a new language is fairly high for most people. It likely will require the following resources: time, mental energy, money.

If time is your scarcest resource, then it will be important to identify small bits of action that will generate progress toward your goal. For example, perhaps the smallest bit would be to review a single word via audio 5 times per day. This small bit is something that can be accomplished on even the most time constrained days. On days with more time, perhaps the task is to listen to 15 minutes of audio in the given language.

By reducing the desired activity into small bits, it becomes easier to create a habit. As the habit is created, it becomes easier to increase the bits into larger pieces of activity. After identifying the bit-sized actions for your goal, it's time to design successful prompts, or triggers, in order to catalyze action.

Chapter 3: How to Design Effective Triggers

"Man is largely a creature of habit, and many of his activities are more or less automatic reflexes from the stimuli of his environment."
-G. Stanley Hall, American Psychologist

Inaction breeds doubt and fear. Action breeds confidence and courage. If you want to conquer fear, do not sit home and think about it. Go out and get busy."
-Dale Carnegie

All of us have triggers in our life that prompt action. Some of these triggers are biological (hunger, thirst, sex). Other triggers are habitual or routine (alcohol or drug use, watching TV after work, getting angry when someone cuts you off in traffic). Other triggers may be based on emotions (when I am bored I will find food to eat, when I am angry I will yell at someone). For most, the triggers are developed unintentionally, and left in the unconscious mind.

This unintentional development of triggers is normal, as it begins in early childhood. Children observe the world and soak in as much information as possible in order to learn how to survive and live. Patterns emerge, cause and effect is learned. As this happens, triggers are programmed into the mind. These triggers and actions all served a purpose at one point. However, many of them are likely no longer helping you reach your goals. Or perhaps your goals have shifted, but your triggers haven't changed yet.

Also, the word 'trigger' often has a negative connotation associated with it. This is especially true in the case of trauma. However I intentionally use the word here because what happens in the brain is exactly the same with negative triggers and positive triggers. All triggers are created by the brain as a way to accomplish some goal - though as mentioned before, many triggers are created unconsciously.

As an example, perhaps you went through what seemed like a traumatic life experience as a child and broke your arm falling off something tall. This could create an unconscious trigger in your body and mind that looks something like this:

- When I am up high, I get hurt and break my arm
- I don't want to break my arm or get hurt
- Give feeling of dizziness or fear when up high to avoid getting hurt in future

In this instance, the trigger (or prompt) is heights, and the feeling is fear or dizziness. This trigger was created unconsciously by the body and mind as an attempt to protect. This trigger can also be changed as the mind learns new information, or realizes old information is no longer relevant due to new experience.

It doesn't necessarily matter what triggers you currently have or how you got them. What matters is the decision to consciously make new triggers that replace and override the old ones that are no longer helping you. This transformation is healing and empowering as you rid yourself of old triggers and create new ones. The transformation of triggers is possible because of a concept called neuroplasticity.

Neuroplasticity and the Brain

Neuroplasticity is an empowering scientific concept about the brain. In simple terms, neuroplasticity states that no matter what patterns your brain learned, they can be overwritten. The brain is constantly changing. This is true if you are 16 or 60. Don't believe me? Think of someone you know who went through what might be considered a "traumatic event" that changed them. It doesn't matter how old they are - they *changed*. This happens because shocking events often cause people to rewrite scripts (programming) in their brains in order to cope with their new concept of how life works.

This can also happen in the positive - and importantly, it can happen intentionally. Because of neuroplasticity, it is possible for you to find old triggers, and map new actions on top of them. It is also possible to design entirely new triggers and map new behaviors on top of them.

In order to better understand this concept, consider the trigger of hunger. For most people, the feeling of hunger is a trigger to go find food. This is a biological survival trigger. However, if you are 50 pounds overweight, perhaps the hunger trigger is something you could learn to map a new behavior onto in order to become more healthy. Now in order to map a new behavior, start by clearly defining both the current trigger and the desired action.

>Using the example above:
>>*Trigger*: Hunger
>>*Old Action*: Go to fridge and eat
>>*Desired New Action*: Drink a glass of water, then set a timer for 15 minutes before eating

There are a number of different behaviors you could design around this trigger in order to promote the goal of reducing body fat in order to increase your physical health.

All behavior boils down to this:

Trigger → Action. Trigger → Action. Trigger → Action.

>Remember, not all triggers are designed intentionally. However when you have a desire to change your behavior, it is important to identify triggers that you can anchor the new behavior to.

Some of the best triggers are things that you are already doing habitually, such as brushing your teeth or taking a shower.

When you decide to make an already habitual action (such as brushing your teeth) a trigger, it becomes very easy to incorporate a new behavior (like doing a set of pushups) immediately following that action. This can be thought of as "habit stacking." You are stacking a new habit on top of an old one.

Brush my teeth → Set of pushups. Brush my teeth → Set of pushups. Brush my teeth → Set of pushups.

Over and over and over, until the pushups become a new habit.

Remember that when starting a new action that is not yet a habit, motivation will wax and wane. Because of this, it is important to break down your new action into small bits. These bits should be actions that *lead into* the main action, but that can be done when your motivation (or resources) are temporarily lower.

For example, a well-designed prompt (trigger) and action plan might look something like this:

Goal: Reduce body fat
Trigger: Brush my teeth
Full Action: Do a set of pushups
Bit-sized action: Do at least one set of pushups from my knees
Smaller bit-sized action: Do at least one pushup from my knees

When motivation and ability are both low, doing a set of pushups might sound daunting. However doing at least one pushup, from your knees. Well, you can do at least that tonight - no matter what.

The smallest bit-sized action should be something that is incredibly easy to accomplish, but still moves you toward your goal and toward your desired full action. Here is another example:

Goal: Run a marathon
Trigger: Get home from work
Full Action: Run X miles
Bit-sized Action: Run around the block

Smaller bit-sized action: Put on my running shoes, start listening to my running music, and go outside

The smaller bit-sized action leads into the bit-sized action, which in turn leads into the full action. The goal is to give your brain something so easy to focus on, that you can *at least* do that. Then, once the smaller bit-sized action is accomplished, you might find yourself moving naturally into the bit-sized action, which will naturally lead you into the full action.

Action breeds action.

Success breeds success.

Movement breeds movement.

Trigger → Action. Trigger → Action. Trigger → Action.

Chapter 4: Just Add One

"The most important step a man can take. It's not the first one, is it? It's the next one. Always the next step."
- Brandon Sanderson

"Rome wasn't built in a day, and neither is your body."
-Tony Horton

As you incorporate the principles explained in the previous chapters, the keystone that holds it all together is this: just add one. Set your goals. Determine your lead measures. Design your triggers. Discipline yourself to complete your lead measure task each day (or multiple times a day). Over time, just add one.

The power of adding one is enormous. Imagine you have $1,000 to your name. What happens if you grow your net worth by 1% every day for a year? By the end of the year your net worth will have increased to over $37,000. Do that again for another year and your net worth will be over $1,400,000.

Maybe money isn't what drives you. Maybe it's physical fitness. You have a goal to increase the amount of weight you can bench press or squat. Every week, just add one pound to the bar (ok, technically 2.5 pound plates are the smallest you can add, so 5 pounds each month instead of one pound each week). By the end of a year, you will have increased the weight that you can bench or squat by 60 pounds! Or maybe you want to do 50 pull ups in a set. Every week, just add one.

The idea is simple. It works. Oftentimes the most difficult thing to do is just get started. Once a task has begun, you start building momentum, and the momentum helps push you forward. So rather than think about your goal of being a multi-millionaire in 5 years, just add one today.

Clearly for some goals, you won't be able to add one every single day. It might be every week, or every 10 days. Find out what interval works for you and your goal, and stick to it. The most important thing is to do the work daily and consistently and intentionally.

This is perhaps the holy grail to all improvement in life. Just add one. That's it. One. Whatever your goal is, start where you are, and just add one. We build habits and lifestyles the same way a wall is built: one brick at a time. Thinking of the end goal can be daunting. So rather than starting with the end, start with the beginning. Start with just adding one. Then a few days later, add one more.

The power behind this is a mixture of many of the concepts discussed in this book so far. First, it reduces the ability required for the task. By reducing the ability, it makes it easy to perform each day - even on days where you don't have as much motivation. Next, it gets you in the habit of *doing*. Action breeds action. Momentum breeds momentum. Just take the next step. If you meditated for 3 minutes last night, you can meditate for 3 minutes tonight. Finally, it is task-oriented. No ego. Just a simple task.

You will notice that by doing this, you set yourself up to win. No herculean effort required. There are two major reasons this is vitally important. First, it will build confidence in your ability to do. Second, it helps the brain reinforce a new neural pathway, which will turn the new action into a habit. When you just add one, you allow yourself room to grow.

Now that you have the principles down - it's time to move on to the worksheets. The worksheets will briefly review the principles as you go through them - but again, the book was designed to be short. This makes it easy to quickly reference a specific chapter in order to refresh the concepts in it. As you begin this journey toward your goals, - I wish you all the happiness and success in the world. It's out there - waiting for you to claim it. Now, just add one.

Chapter 5: The Worksheets

Re-Define your Goals

Concepts to remember:
- Set goals in each of the following categories, but only work on 1-2 per quarter: Physical, spiritual, social, mental, financial
- Use the "Be Do Have" method to help brainstorm goals if you aren't sure where to start
- Set goals in the following format: From X to Y by Date. This keeps you accountable to a specific time frame and gives you something to measure against. Example: From $1,000 in savings to $5,000 in savings by March 30th.
- Set TASK-oriented goals rather than EGO-oriented goals. This keeps the goal more within your control. It is also significantly more measurable.
- Use the WOOP method to plan for obstacles that would have kept you from reaching your goal, had you not planned for it in advance.

- Identify LEAD measures (or leading indicators) that, if done consistently, will accurately predict that you reach your goal (the LAG measure).

In the spaces below, write down a few goals that you have in each category. Focus on "Be Do Have"

Example

Physical: Be in peak physical condition. Have a visible six pack. Do a triathlon.
Spiritual: Be more kind. Have more compassion for those who are in less fortunate circumstances than myself. Meditate daily.
Mental: Be an expert in machine learning. Get a PhD in Computer Science. Read one book a month.
Social: Be more outgoing. Have more close friends. Take swing dancing lessons.
Financial: Be financially independent. Own a Tesla Cyber Truck. Start my own business for extra income.

Now, list your first set of goals:

Physical:

_____
_____
_____
_____
_____

Spiritual:

_____
_____
_____
_____
_____

Mental:

_____
_____
_____
_____
_____

Social:

_____
_____
_____

_____
_____

Financial:

_____
_____
_____
_____
_____

Next, examine the list above and ask yourself the following: which one (or two) of these goals, if I could accomplish it immediately in this instant, would have the biggest positive impact on my life? Don't spend too much time thinking - just choose the one or two that immediately jump out at you. Write them down here:

<u>Example</u>

Start a side business for extra income.
Meditate daily.

Goal One:

_____
_____
_____

_____

Goal Two:

_____
_____
_____

_____

These will be the goals that you focus on for the next period of time. I recommend at least 3 months.

Now format the goals as follows:
> From X to Y by Date

This is where you should get more specific about the goals. What is it you really want? Is it a side business that sucks away your time but doesn't pay you anything? Of course not. You want a business that gives you extra money at the end of every month.

Example

Go from $0/mo. in my side business to $300/mo. by March 30th.

Go from 0 minutes of daily meditation to 15 minutes of daily meditation by March 30th.

Goal One (From X to Y by When):

_____
_____
_____

_____

Goal Two (From X to Y by When):

_____
_____
_____

_____

First state where you currently are, then where you would like to be. Last, establish the date that the goal will be accomplished by. Now you are ready to find some leading indicators.

With each goal, think of two or three things that, if done consistently, will lead to the greatest chance of success with this goal. These should be task-oriented items that are within your control. These will be tied into designing triggers and designing your scoreboard. So give some careful thought to them.

<u>Example</u>

Goal One: Go from $0/mo. in my side business to $300/mo. by March 30th.
>**Lead indicator one:** Research 3 potential business ideas each day until I decide what kind of business I want to start
>**Lead indicator two:** Do three social media posts per day for my new business
>**Lead indicator three:** Create one new ad campaign each week

Goal One

    Lead indicator one:

_____

    Lead indicator two:

_____

    Lead indicator three:

_____

Goal Two

    Lead indicator one:

_____

    Lead indicator two:

_____

    Lead indicator three:

_____

For each goal, go through the WOOP process. The Obstacle + Plan should be repeated for each lead indicator. There could also be more obstacles that you think of.

<u>Example</u>

Goal One: Go from $0/mo. in my side business to $300/mo. by March 30th.

Wish: I build up my side business to the point that it replaces my current income

Outcome: I will have more financial flexibility, freedom of time, freedom to travel, and the ability to scale my business in order to achieve financial independence.

Obstacle: My paid ads might not perform well.

Plan: I can watch YouTube videos or find some courses online that teach how to do it. Or I can outsource the ads to someone on Upwork / Fiverr.

Obstacle: I might get home from work and feel too tired to work on a side business.

Plan: On days that I feel too tired after work, I will set a 30 minute timer as soon as I get home from work. For those 30 minutes I will relax and decompress. Then when the timer goes off, I will start working on my side business for at least 30 minutes.

Obstacle: My wife/husband/boyfriend/girlfriend/children might feel like the extra business is pulling my time away from them.

Plan: I will do what I can to invite my wife/husband/boyfriend/girlfriend/children to help me with the business so we can be spending time together while building financial security.

Goal One

Wish:
_____

Outcome:
_____

Obstacle:
_____

Plan:
_____

Obstacle:
_____

Plan:
_____

Obstacle:
_____

Plan:
_____

Goal Two

Wish:
_____

Outcome:
_____

Obstacle:
_____

Plan:
_____

Obstacle:
_____

Plan:
_____

Obstacle:
_____

Plan:
_____

This concludes the end of the goal-setting action items. Now it's time to take those goals, and design daily triggers that will help you reach them.

Action Item: Design your Triggers

Concepts to remember:
- Triggers can be consciously designed, though most go through life only forming triggers unconsciously.
- Triggers should be something that is already happening on a regular basis. Such as showering, brushing your teeth, or getting a text message. This is also called habit stacking.
- Tie lead measures to the triggers. Something that you can do every day that will predict the eventual success of your goal.
- Start where you are with the lead measure. Just add one as you go.

Action Item: Build Your Scoreboard

Key items of an effective scoreboard:

- Frequently visible (on your bathroom mirror, fridge, desktop, etc.)
- Easy to see progress of lead and lag measures at a glance
- Easy to update
- Shared with accountability partner

One of the easiest (and free!) places to build a scoreboard is using Google Sheets. They don't look super pretty, but it hits all of the criteria very well. Here is an example:

	A	B	C	D	E	F	G
1	Goal	Go from 25 to 100 Military Pushups by Dec 31 2021					
2	Lead Measure	Set Max pushups 3x/day					
3	Trigger	Eating Breakfast, Lunch, and Dinner					
4	Action	Before eating breakfast, lunch, or dinner, do one set of max pushups with strict form					
5	Smaller Action	Do at least 25 pushups					
6	Bit Sized Action	Do at least 1 pushup					
7		Date					
8	**Triggers**	10/25	10/26	10/27	10/28	10/29 . . . 12/31	
9	Breakfast	75	75	76	80	77	100
10	Lunch	75	75	75	76	77	100
11	Dinner	75	75	76	76	77	100

Notice that in addition to having the end goal, the sheet also clearly identifies lead measures, actions, and gives an "at a glance" view of progress being made over time. Additionally, it is very easy to share a google sheet with an accountability partner who can see your progress and cheer you on.

Also, it is very easy to use google sheets to create a blank template that can be printed out and updated by hand. Or if you would prefer, you can go to www.tylertaggart.com/scoreboard to print out a free version of our scoreboard, or get a Just Add One Quarterly Planner at www.tylertaggart.com/QuarterlyPlanner that has built in scoreboards.

Resources

Fogg, BJ. (2020). The Fogg Behavioral Model. https://behaviormodel.org/

Huling, J., McChesney, C., and Covey, S. (2012). *The 4 Disciplines of Execution*. Free Press. https://www.franklincovey.com/the-4-disciplines/

Manning, C. (2010). *The Fearless Mind: 5 Essential Steps to High Performance*. Cedar Fort, Inc. https://thefearlessmind.com/

Oettingen, G. (2014). *Rethinking Positive Thinking: Inside the New Science of Motivation*. Penguin Books. https://woopmylife.org/en/science

Robbins, T. (1992). *Awaken the Giant Within: How to Take Immediate Control of Your Mental, Emotional, Physical and Financial Destiny!* Simon and Schuester. http://core.tonyrobbins.com/atgw-ebook

Because Amazon requires 72 pages for a physical print on demand book, here are some additional worksheets to use.

Identify 10 Wildly Important Goals

Physical | Social | Spiritual | Financial | Mental

1. _____
2. _____
3. _____
4. _____
5. _____
6. _____
7. _____
8. _____
9. _____
10. _____

Which goal, if it was
already accomplished now,
would have the biggest positive impact on
your life? (go with your gut reaction)

Translate the goal: From X to Y by: Date

For Example: I will go from 220 lbs to 200 lbs body weight by losing 20 lbs of fat by Dec 31st

Translated Wildly IMPORTANT! Goal

_____

_____

_____

Establish Lead Measures

What measurable activities will predict hitting your goal?
For example: goal: lose fat - measure: minutes of exercise
Rate how you are already doing on each (1 to 10)

1. _____
2. _____
3. _____
4. _____
5. _____

Which one or two activities are the
"highest leverage" activities?
Which two, if performed consistently, will
give you the biggest bang for your buck?

Desired Outcomes

When you accomplish this goal, how will you feel? How will your life change?

1. _____

   _____

2. _____

   _____

3. _____

   _____

4. _____

   _____

5. _____

   _____

Obstacles and Plans

For your lead measure (or measures), what are some realistic potential obstacles that might make it difficult to accomplish? What is your plan when this obstacle comes up?

Obstacle:

_____
_____

Plan:

_____
_____

Obstacle:

_____
_____

Plan:

_____
_____

12 Week Scoreboard

From _____ to _____ by _____

Lead Measure One: _____
Lead Measure Two: _____

1	2	3	4	5	6	7
8	9	10	11	12	13	14
15	16	17	18	19	20	21
22	23	24	25	26	27	28

1	2	3	4	5	6	7
8	9	10	11	12	13	14
15	16	17	18	19	20	21
22	23	24	25	26	27	28

1	2	3	4	5	6	7
8	9	10	11	12	13	14
15	16	17	18	19	20	21
22	23	24	25	26	27	28

Identify 10 Wildly Important Goals

Physical | Social | Spiritual | Financial | Mental

1. _____
2. _____
3. _____
4. _____
5. _____
6. _____
7. _____
8. _____
9. _____
10. _____

Which goal, if it was
already accomplished now,
would have the biggest positive impact on
your life? (go with your gut reaction)

Translate the goal: From X to Y by: Date

For Example: I will go from 220 lbs to 200 lbs body weight by losing 20 lbs of fat by Dec 31st

Establish Lead Measures

What measurable activities will predict hitting your goal?
For example: goal: lose fat - measure: minutes of exercise
Rate how you are already doing on each (1 to 10)

1. _____
2. _____
3. _____
4. _____
5. _____

Which one or two activities are the
"highest leverage" activities?
Which two, if performed consistently, will
give you the biggest bang for your buck?

Desired Outcomes

When you accomplish this goal, how will you feel? How will your life change?

1. _____
   _____
2. _____
   _____
3. _____
   _____
4. _____
   _____
5. _____
   _____

Obstacles and Plans

For your lead measure (or measures), what are some realistic potential obstacles that might make it difficult to accomplish? What is your plan when this obstacle comes up?

Obstacle:
_____
_____

Plan:
_____
_____

Obstacle:
_____
_____

Plan:
_____
_____

12 Week Scoreboard

From _____ to _____ by _____

Lead Measure One: _____
Lead Measure Two: _____

1	2	3	4	5	6	7
8	9	10	11	12	13	14
15	16	17	18	19	20	21
22	23	24	25	26	27	28

1	2	3	4	5	6	7
8	9	10	11	12	13	14
15	16	17	18	19	20	21
22	23	24	25	26	27	28

1	2	3	4	5	6	7
8	9	10	11	12	13	14
15	16	17	18	19	20	21
22	23	24	25	26	27	28

Identify 10 Wildly Important Goals

Physical | Social | Spiritual | Financial | Mental

1. _____
2. _____
3. _____
4. _____
5. _____
6. _____
7. _____
8. _____
9. _____
10. _____

Which goal, if it was
already accomplished now,
would have the biggest positive impact on
your life? (go with your gut reaction)

Translate the goal: From X to Y by: Date

For Example: I will go from 220 lbs to 200 lbs body weight by losing 20 lbs of fat by Dec 31st

Establish Lead Measures

What measurable activities will predict hitting your goal?
For example: goal: lose fat - measure: minutes of exercise
Rate how you are already doing on each (1 to 10)

1. _____
2. _____
3. _____
4. _____
5. _____

Which one or two activities are the
"highest leverage" activities?
Which two, if performed consistently, will
give you the biggest bang for your buck?

Desired Outcomes

When you accomplish this goal, how will you feel? How will your life change?

1. _____
   _____
2. _____
   _____
3. _____
   _____
4. _____
   _____
5. _____
   _____

Obstacles and Plans

For your lead measure (or measures), what are some realistic potential obstacles that might make it difficult to accomplish? What is your plan when this obstacle comes up?

Obstacle:

Plan:

Obstacle:

Plan:

----

12 Week Scoreboard

From _____ to _____ by _____

Lead Measure One: _____
Lead Measure Two: _____

1	2	3	4	5	6	7
8	9	10	11	12	13	14
15	16	17	18	19	20	21
22	23	24	25	26	27	28

1	2	3	4	5	6	7
8	9	10	11	12	13	14
15	16	17	18	19	20	21
22	23	24	25	26	27	28

1	2	3	4	5	6	7
8	9	10	11	12	13	14
15	16	17	18	19	20	21
22	23	24	25	26	27	28

Made in the USA
Coppell, TX
07 January 2022